SERMONS

SERMONS

(For Beginners, Lay Speakers,
Motivational Speakers, Pastors, and Leaders)

World-Renowned Author
Melissa Weeks-Richardson

Copyright © 2018 by Melissa Weeks-Richardson.

Library of Congress Control Number: 2018906079
ISBN: Hardcover   978-1-9845-2959-6
               Softcover   978-1-9845-2958-9
               eBook   978-1-9845-2957-2

All rights reserved. No part of this book may be reproduced or transmitted in any form or by any means, electronic or mechanical, including photocopying, recording, or by any information storage and retrieval system, without permission in writing from the copyright owner.

NIV

Scripture quotations marked NIV are taken from the Holy Bible, New International Version®. NIV®. Copyright © 1973, 1978, 1984 by International Bible Society. Used by permission of Zondervan. All rights reserved. [Biblica]

KJV

Scripture quotations marked KJV are from the Holy Bible, King James Version (Authorized Version). First published in 1611. Quoted from the KJV Classic Reference Bible, Copyright © 1983 by The Zondervan Corporation.

Any people depicted in stock imagery provided by Getty Images are models, and such images are being used for illustrative purposes only.
Certain stock imagery © Getty Images.

Print information available on the last page.

Rev. date: 05/18/2018

To order additional copies of this book, contact:
Xlibris
1-888-795-4274
www.Xlibris.com
Orders@Xlibris.com
779422

CONTENTS

Preface vii

Don't Quit 1
Tried in the Fire . . . Coming Out Gold 5
Praise Him Anyhow 9
Where Are You Casting Your Net? 15
Stand Still 19
Trust in the Lord with All Your Heart................................ 21
No Condemnation 25
Will You Be Ready When Jesus Comes?............................ 29
Wake Up 33
The Earth Is the Lord's 35
What Kind of Legacy Are You Leaving Behind? 37
Every Knee Shall Bow 41
Let This Mind Be in You 43
The Lord Is a Refuge... 45
Remembering the Golden Rule 47
What Kind of Inheritance Are You Leaving Behind?......51
The Love of God 55
A Merry Heart: Get Your Joy Back..................................... 59
How Bad Do You Want It? 63

References 67

PREFACE

THE SERMONS IN this book are just a few of my many sermons that God allowed me to preach over the last twelve years. God instructed me to put them in a book. "Don't Quit" was my initial sermon. There are times I find myself watching and listening to other sermons for encouragement or just because I have been inspired by certain preachers. Oftentimes, I listen to my bishop's sermons.

These sermons may inspire or encourage you. God may even give you a revelation or a sermon from a sermon. These sermons are not just for beginners. They are also for lay speakers, motivational speakers, pastors, and other leaders.

DON'T QUIT

Text: 1 Corinthians 9: 19–27
Author: Paul
Date: Written about AD 59

History

HERE, WE SEE that Paul is saying in a sense that he was free from all men. He is encouraging one to live free from all obligations to men. However, serve as if you are a personal slave. *Slave* is defined according to *Webster's Standard Dictionary* as "one owned by another, one completely subject to another or to some habit or influence, a device controlled by another device or to toil ceaselessly."

According to the text, he made himself a servant unto all that he might gain more. No one could exercise jurisdiction or compulsion over him. According to the text, he brought himself under bondage that he might win more. *Bondage* is defined by Nelson as "subjection to oppression." He was willing to eat foods Jewish people ate and refrained from eating things such as pork, which was forbidden. He also refrained from working on the Sabbath. He realized that if he did this, the Gospel might gain more hearing. Those who had scruples (reluctance by disapproval) and those weak in the faith do not cause to stumble by doing those things, which would violate their weak conscience (Romans

14:1–15). Paul did everything in his power to be like those he tried to win, except enter into sin with them.

How many of us are willing to do this today? How many of us are willing to live for God, taking the limits off Him and allowing Him to have His way in our lives and do whatever is necessary or go the extra mile for the benefit of spreading the Gospel if it would mean winning souls for the kingdom?

First Timothy 6:11 tells us to follow after righteousness, godliness, faith, love, patience, and meekness (KJV). When running in a race, not all will receive the prize, only the winner. This Christian journey is like a race. It requires self-discipline. We see that the prize on this Christian journey is not salvation but a reward for our faithful service. Salvation is a gift that was freely given by God, and it is through faith in the Lord Jesus. This is something that cannot be earned.

When we look at verse 25, it mentions a perishable crown—a garland of flowers or a wreath of leaves that will soon wither away. It is something that will not last.

The commentator stated that an imperishable crown is a crown that will be awarded to all who have been faithful in their service to Christ. An imperishable crown is a crown that will last.

If I can leave you with a message, it would be "Don't quit."

On this Christian journey, we will have some trials and tribulations, but just don't quit. Trials will come, but they come to make you strong. Surely, while running this race, you are going to find yourself running alone, but don't quit.

Remember, Paul made himself a servant unto all that he might gain more. So while you are running, you might find yourself running with some haters, but don't quit. You find yourself running with people who will scandalize your name, but don't quit. You may have to run with lepers, but don't quit. You may have to run with liars and backbiters, but don't quit. You may have to run with individuals who don't want to run with you, but don't quit. You will have to endure hardship along the way, but just don't quit. Keep your eyes on the prize, and don't quit. The same way Paul made himself a servant unto all that he might gain more, you have to make up your mind that you will be like Paul and say, "Come what may, but I am not going to quit."

TRIED IN THE FIRE... COMING OUT GOLD

Text: Daniel 3:16–27
Author: Daniel (a captive prince from Judah, an interpreter of dreams and visions, a prime minister under several kings, and a prophet of God)
Date and place: Written from Babylon and Sushan about 606 or 616 to 536 BC

History

HERE, WE ARE dealing with Daniel's friends being tested in the fiery furnace. It was here that Nebuchadnezzar, the king, made an image of gold.

Who was Nebuchadnezzar?
- His name means "nebo, defend the boundary."
- He was the son of Nabopolassar.
- He was the king of Babylon.
- He became prominent in scripture in the history of the chastening of Judah by God.

Babylon

According to the *Thompson Chain Reference Bible*, Babylon was the mightiest city of the ancient world. It was largely built by the efforts of Hammurabi (1728–1686 BC) and Nebuchadnezzar II (604–562 BC). It declined with the fall of Nebuchadnezzar to a lower level under Belshazzar and came to ruin about 130 BC at the hands of Parthians.

My Bible tells me that Nebuchadnezzar gathered eight main classes to come to the dedication of the image he set up, and in those classes were the following:

1. Princes—These are found to be the satraps or privy counselors who had access to the king at all times.
2. Governors—These were the lieutenants, the viceroys, and the nobles of various provinces.
3. Captains—In this category were pashas, deputy rulers of outlying provinces, and leaders of armies.
4. Judges—Here, we had assistants to the king in making laws.
5. Treasurers—These were those in charge of the treasure houses.
6. Counselors—This group consisted of supreme masters and civil magistrates.
7. Sheriffs—This group consisted of supreme masters and civil magistrates.
8. Rulers of provinces—This group consisted of state and civil offers and various wise men.

In the text, we also see that a herald read a decree that was sent out by the king. A herald was someone employed by kings to announce decrees and proclaim their coming. The decree stated that at the time they heard the cornet, flute, harp, sackbut (a type of harp), psaltery (a stringed instrument), and dulcimer (a tambourine or tom-tom drum)—all kinds of music—they were to fall down and worship the golden image.

Nelson's Three-in-One Bible Reference Companion defines *worship* as "an expression of the relationship between believers and God, involving reference and adoration of God, devotion to false gods."

Whoever did not follow this decree, whoever did not fall down and worship the golden image would be cast in the midst of the burning furnace. There were three Jews (friends of Daniel):

- Shadrach—His original name was Hananiah, which means "gift of the Lord." He was renamed Shadrach, meaning "command of Aku, the moon god."
- Meshach—His original name was Mishael, which means "who is what God is." He was renamed Meshach, meaning "who is as Aku."
- Abednego—His original name was Azariah, which means "Jehovah helps." He was renamed to Abednego, meaning "servant of Nebo, the god of science and literature."

These three refused, and because they refused, they were thrown into a fiery furnace, which was turned up seven times hotter. The furnace was so hot that it slew the men that took up Shadrach, Meshach, and Abednego. However, they were not harmed; the hairs on their head were not singed, nor were their garments affected. They did not even smell like smoke.

My message to you is this: "You have been tried in the fire, but you are coming out gold."

Have you ever felt like you have been thrown into a fiery furnace that was turned up seven times hotter because you refused to bow down and worship man's golden image?

Were you thrown into a furnace because you refused to bow down and worship your job? Did you refuse to follow the crowd? Did you refuse to follow the traditional way of doing things? Have you ever refused to give up your right for someone else's wrong? Were you thrown in the fiery furnace for standing up for what was right?

If you fall in one of these categories, then I need to let you know that the same way God delivered Shadrach, Meshach, and Abednego, He can deliver you. God sees you, and He knows exactly where you are at this point and time. Just hold on. He sees your tears. He can hear your cries. He sees your faithfulness. He hears your prayers.

Because of your faithfulness, because you stand on the Word, because of your refusal to give up, because of your refusal to bow down to man, because of your refusal to follow man's tradition, because of your willingness to do what is right instead of what is wrong, because of your refusal to follow the crowd, God is going to step into your situation. God is going to bring you out. When He brings you out, you will be pure as God.

Authentic gold has to be purified. According to *Encyclopedia Britannica*, gold (ace) melts at a temperature of 1,064 degrees Celsius (1,947 degrees Fahrenheit). You may be tried in the fire, but you are coming out gold. Remain in the fire, and let God purify you. You are being authenticated.

PRAISE HIM ANYHOW

Text: Acts 16:16–26
Author: Luke (the beloved physician)
Date written: Written about AD 63 in an unknown place

History

THIS SECTION DEALS with a fortune-telling demon being cast out by Paul and Silas. This caused them to be thrown in jail. Paul and Silas were, according to the text, on their way to prayer. They were on their way to a place of worship. While on their way, they were met by a damsel, which is defined by *Nelson's Three-in-One Bible Reference* as "a young woman who was possessed with a spirit of divination" (v. 16).

The spirit of divination is an attempt to foretell the unknown by occult means (*Nelson's*, 192). In Greek, according to *Dake's Study Bible*, this is also known as the spirit of the python or Apollo's python. According to fable, it was a huge serpent that had an oracle on Mt. Parnassus. It was famous for predicting future events. He further states that Apollo slew this serpent and was called Pytheus, becoming celebrated as the fortune-teller of events. It was believed that all who pretended to fortune-tell events were influenced by the spirit of Apollo Pytheus. A priestess at his temple was called Pythoness, and it was through her that messages were delivered.

According to the text, this damsel brought her masters much gain by soothsaying (fortune-telling). A *soothsayer*, according to *Webster's Dictionary*, is "one who claims to be able to foretell the future." She followed Paul and cried, saying, "These men are servants of the Most High God, which show unto us the way of salvation."

The commentator pointed out in the text that every word was true. However, Satan's purpose in it was to discredit the message of the apostles by making the people think they were in a league with demon spirits who were making this announcement through a demon-possessed medium. By doing this, the people would then conclude that they were doing miracles by the devil and discount the Gospel. When the demon was cast out in the name that is above every name, in the name of Jesus, it proved that they were of God, not of demons. The damsel followed them many days, doing this, according to verse 18. This grieved Paul. Why? Because he saw exactly what Satan was doing. He immediately discerned Satan's tactics, and because of this, Paul turned to the demon, not the girl, and commanded it to come out. This was a spirit operating within the girl. Ephesians 6:12 says, "For we wrestle not against flesh and blood, but against principalities, against powers, against rulers of the darkness of this world, against spiritual wickedness in high places" (KJV).

We see here that when Paul commanded that spirit to come out in the name of Jesus, my Bible tells me that it came out that same hour. It did not take days. It did not take weeks. Paul did not have to do any type of rituals. The spirit came out that same hour. This caused a problem for Paul and Silas. When was the last time you stood for Christ and it caused an uproar? When was the last time you stood for Christ and it shut some stuff down?

When her masters saw their gain was gone, this was when they realized it was time to do something. They dragged the apostles before the Roman rulers in the marketplace where they held court according to the commentator. The apostles were taken before the magistrate where they told the magistrates, "These men are Jews do exceedingly trouble our city." Paul was a Benjamite (Philippians 3:5); the others were of other tribes, but all were Jews. They stated that they taught customs that were not lawful for them to receive nor to observe being Romans. According to *Dake's Study Bible*, Romans were very zealous for their national worship. Great care was taken that no one introduced a new religion. Jews were banished from Rome.

We see that magistrates rent off their clothes and commanded to beat the apostles. According to the commentator, to beat with rods was the method of treating a criminal. Jews gave only thirty-nine stripes, but Romans had no such law. They gave as many as they chose. This is referred to by Paul in 2 Corinthians 11:23 as "stripes beyond measure or moderation" (Dake, 143d).

After beating them or laying many stripes on them, they cast them into prison and charged the jailer to keep them safely. Not only were they thrown into prison but they were thrown into an inner prison with their feet fastened into stocks. Roman stocks were made to keep them from escaping. They were made with holes wide enough apart as to stretch legs and bruise the feet to cause pain and injury. This with the stripes made them suffer agony (Dake, 143d). Verse 25 states that at midnight, Paul and Silas were praying and singing hymns and the prisoners were listening to them. Suddenly, there was a great earthquake. So the foundations of the prison were shaken, and immediately, all the doors were opened. And everyone's chains were loose. My message in all this is "Praise Him anyhow."

Have you ever been locked up or ever felt as though you were locked up and could not get out or it looked like you were never going to get out?

You may have been locked up in your finances, locked up in your thoughts, or locked up in sin; maybe you were locked up in some sort of lifestyles that you tried to get out of or were just locked up behind prison walls. If that is you or if you ever find yourself in that situation, don't give up. Don't settle in that situation. Praise Him anyhow. Praise God while you are in the midst.

If you are one that says, I have never experienced anything like this, then I must say to you to keep living because trials are sure to come to everyone. They come to make us strong.

James 1:2–4 says, "My brethren, count it all joy when ye fall into diverse temptations; knowing this that the trying of your faith worketh patience. But let patience have her perfect work, that ye may be perfect and entire wanting nothing" (KJV).

Notice that the scripture in verse 2 says, "Count it all joy when ye fall into diverse temptations." This lets us know that trials are coming. It is just a matter of when. This lets us know that the trying of our faith worketh patience. While you are in the midst of whatever it is that you may be going through, you ought to praise Him anyhow, knowing that something good will come out of it on the other side.

That means that when they talk about you, that is when you have to make up your mind and say, "I'm going to praise Him anyhow."

When that loved one walks out on you, praise Him anyhow. When your family turns their back on you, that is okay. Do not fret because you have already made up your mind that you are going to praise Him anyhow. When your supervisor comes to you on your job at the end of the day telling you that they do not need you any more, there is no need to get discouraged. Just praise Him anyhow. When the doctor comes to you with a bad report or with a false-positive report, you have to be determined that you are going to praise Him anyhow.

Once you have made up your mind that you are going to praise Him anyhow and you continue to praise Him, you will see that foundations begin to shake. Psalm 30:5 says, "Weeping may endure for a night, but joy comes in the morning."

If God could deliver Shadrach, Meshach, and Abednego out of a fiery furnace and Daniel out of the lion's den, just know that He can also deliver you. I also am reminded of a forty-two-year-old woman down in Sumter, South Carolina, who was delivered.

He picked me up and turned me around. He placed my feet on solid ground. No matter where you may find yourself, no matter what you may be going through, just remember to praise Him anyhow.

WHERE ARE YOU CASTING YOUR NET?

Text: John 21:3–6; Deuteronomy 1:6–11
Authors: John (beloved disciple and author of John) and Moses (the law giver and leader of Israel and author of Deuteronomy)
Date written: John was written about AD 90 in an unknown place; Deuteronomy was written about 1645 BC in the plains of Moab by Jordan near Jericho, just before the entrance into Canaan.

History

SIMON AND A few other disciples went fishing. We see that they were fishing apparently at night and caught nothing. According to the commentator, they used the same method that they previously had used when they went on their prior fishing trip. It was here, and in Luke 5:1–11, the disciples received a call to preach. Christ gave them their miraculous catch.

Jesus was waiting for them as they rowed toward shore the next morning, although they did not recognize Him. Perhaps it was still quite dark, or perhaps they were prevented from knowing Him by God's power. (I cannot add or take.) According to *Believer's Bible Commentary*, it was the same as if the Lord asked, "Young men, have you anything to eat?" They were directed to cast the net to the right side of the boat. It shows that when the Lord directs our service, there are no more empty nets. God knows where there are souls ready to be saved, and He is willing to direct us to them if we let Him.

Body

Have you been toiling or stagnated lately?

Webster's Standard Dictionary defines *toil* as "hard, continuous work, exhausting labor, to move or travel with difficulty, weariness, and pain." It also defines *stagnated* as "to cease to run or flow as water or air; to stop developing, growing, progressing or advancing; to become sluggish or dull."

Have you become stagnated on a job or felt like you could not grow anymore? Have you been fishing for something all night, all week, all month, or all year but caught nothing? Have you found yourself saying, "Lord, I'm tired of doing things my way, and now I want to do them your way. But there is something that is keeping me stagnated, and I want to be free. I want to be free to love right, free to worship you in my own way, free to praise you the way I need to praise you to break chains and loosen shackles. I want to praise you and not be judged. I want to be free to tell people about your goodness and mercy"?

Deuteronomy 1:6 says, "The Lord of God spake unto us in Horeb saying, Ye have dwelt long enough on this mount" (KJV). In other words, you have dwelled here long enough. Turn and take your journey. Deuteronomy 1:8 says, "Behold, I have set the land before you: go and possess the land which the Lord swore before your fathers Abraham, Isaac, and Jacob to give unto them and to their seed after them."

Could it be that God have been speaking to you lately and you did not know that it was Him? Sometimes God has to stretch you in some areas to let you know that He wants to take you somewhere else. Sometimes you stop growing in one area because it just may be time to cast your net in another area.

During this process, it may even become uncomfortable, but just know you are in transition. God may just be telling you to cast your net on the other side.

STAND STILL

Text: Deuteronomy 20:1-4
Author: Moses (the lawgiver and leader of Israel)
Date and time: Written about 1645 BC in the plains of Moab by Jordan near Jericho just before the entrance into Canaan.

History

HERE WE SEE that verses 1–3 are commands. This is a preparation for battle. Verse 1 says, "When thou goest out to battle against thine enemies and seest horses, and chariots, and a people more than thou, be not afraid of them: for the Lord thy God is with thee, which brought thee up out of the land of Egypt." Verse 1 starts by saying, "When thou goest to battle." That lets us know that there will be a time that we will have battles on this Christian journey that we will have to fight.

Ephesians 6:12 says, "For we do not wrestle against flesh and blood against powers, against the rulers of darkness of this age, against spiritual hosts of wickedness of the heavenly places." My message to you is "Stand still!"

First Samuel 17:47 says, "Then all this assembly shall know that the Lord does not save with sword and spear; for the battle is the Lord's and he will give you into our hands."

Verse 3 gives another command: "And shall say unto them, hear o Israel, ye approach, this day unto battle against your enemies:

let not your hearts faint, fear not, and do not tremble, neither be ye terrified because of them" (KJV).

Here, we see two times they are told not to be afraid of their enemies and two times they are assured that God will fight for them and give them victory.

Someone may ask the question, Why I should not be afraid? My response is "Because greater is He that is in you than he that is in the world." My message to you is "Stand still." God will fight for your battles, for the battle is not yours; it belongs to the Lord. Through that sickness you have been dealing with, those unruly children, that addiction, that marital problem, that strife in your family, that depression, those satanic attacks, or whatever it is that you have been battling, just stand still and let God fight for you.

TRUST IN THE LORD WITH ALL YOUR HEART

Text: Proverbs 3:5-8
Author: Solomon
Date written: With the exception of chapters 30–31, the proverbs were spoken by Solomon about 1000 BC. Chapters 1–24 were perhaps written by him in a book. Chapters 25–29 were Solomon's proverbs added to the first part of the book by Hezekiah about 730 BC. The last two chapters were added at an unknown time.

Background

WILLIAM MCDONALD STATES the following:

> To know God's will for your life, there must first be a full commitment of ourselves, which would consist of spirit, soul, and body to the Lord. We must trust him not only for the salvation of our souls but the direction of our lives. We have to know that we do not know what is best for ourselves. We are capable of guiding ourselves. There must be an acknowledgement of the Lordship of Christ. Every areas of our life must be turned over to him. We have been commanded to trust in the Lord with all our heart.

That means to put all our trust in Him—not partial trust but full trust. He is to be given our whole heart. All trust has to be placed in the Lord, not in ourselves. All trust has to be placed in the Lord, not in things. All trust has to be placed in the Lord, not in our government. We say that we trust in God to a certain extent. It is easy to say that we trust in Him as long as we can see His hand moving. As long as we can see things with our natural eyes, we do not have problems with trusting in God. What about the things we cannot see? What about the things we cannot understand? Why try to understand things that you cannot understand?

Let God work things out. When we try to handle things based on our own knowledge and our own skills, that is when we begin to mess up. Step back, and let God be in control. We have been commanded to acknowledge God in all our ways. In every step we take, we are to acknowledge God. We can do nothing without Him.

When we acknowledge God, He will direct our path. We are not to be wise in our own eyes. We are to fear the Lord. In other words, reverence Him. There is a lack of reverence for God today, even in the house of worship. Today, people are saying and doing anything, telling themselves they are big and bold enough to do without any respect. Some live any kind of way.

Our bodies are temples where the Holy Spirit dwells, and we should not just put anything in them. It is not what goes inside that defiles it; it is what comes out of the mouth. (I know that is paraphrasing it.) We have been commanded to depart from evil, to shun it, and to stay away from all appearances of evil. Sometimes that may mean turning away from certain people. That may mean changing certain places you hang out. You don't have to stop talking to your friends, but you may have to let them know in a nice way. "I can't go to those places with you anymore" or "I cannot do those things with you anymore because I am trying to live a holy life."

You may have to ask God to help you. God did not say you cannot have any fun. Sure, you can have fun. He also said, "If your conscience doesn't condemn you, neither will I." He also told us that there will be some who will not inherit the kingdom of God. Let us make sure we are reverencing God. The Word said, "It shall be health to thy navel and marrow to thy bones." When we look back at the text, William McDowell said something that was so profound. He said this:

> When we look at the word Navel and when we know that it is through the navel where the child receives life and nourishment from the mother while that unborn child is inside of the mother's womb. That is the same as fearing God and departing from evil; it gives life to the child of God. By marrow, the bones are being kept moistened, nourished, and not so brittle are less likely to break.

NO CONDEMNATION

Text: Romans 8:1
Author: Paul
Date and time: Sixth of Paul's letters from Corinth about AD 58–60 and sent to Rome by Phoebe.

Scripture

There is therefore now no condemnation to them which are in Christ Jesus who walk not after the flesh but after the Spirit.

—Romans 8:1 (KJV)

Background

MATTHEW HENRY STATED, "The apostle began with one signal privilege of true Christians and describes the character of those to whom it belongs." This is his triumph after the melancholy complaint and conflict in the foregoing chapter—sin remaining, disturbing, vexing, but, blessed be to God, not ruining.

The complaint he takes to himself, but he humbly transfers the comfort with himself to all true believers who are interested in it. He is not saying that there is no accusation against them, but what he is saying is that the accusation is thrown out. He is not saying that there is nothing in them that deserves condemnation, for there is. They see it and own it and mourn over it and condemn themselves for it, but it shall not be to their ruin. They may be chastened by the Lord, but they are not condemned with the world. They are in Christ Jesus. They are protected from the avenger of blood. Christ does not condemn them, but He is pleased with them. In other words, there is no divine condemnation as far as sin is concerned because we are in Christ (to those that are in Christ). And because we are in Christ, we are free from condemnation. We are also free from self-condemnation. The Holy Spirit supplies the risen life of the Lord Jesus, which makes us free from the law of sin and death.

We are not under the law; we are under grace. Under the law, people could not fulfill sacred requirements. Grace succeeds where the law fails. The law could not produce holy living because it was weak through the flesh. The law spoke to men who were already sinners, who could not obey but God.

We see God stepped in and sent His own son, Jesus, in His likeness. Jesus did not come in sinful flesh but in the likeness of sinful flesh. In 1 Peter 2:22, it says, "Who did no sin neither was guile found in his mouth" (KJV). Second Corinthians 5:21 further goes on to state, "For He hath made him to be sin for us, who knew no sin, that we might be made the righteousness of God in him" (KJV). However, it did not stop there. First John 3:5 says, "And that ye know that he was manifested to take away our sins and in him is no sin" (KJV).

By Him coming into the world in human form, He resembled sinful humanity. As a sacrifice for sin, Christ condemned sin in the flesh. Jesus died not only for sins, which we commit, but also for our sinful nature.

First Peter 3:18 says, "For Christ also hath once suffered for sins, the unjust that he might bring us to God, being put to death in the flesh, but quicken by the spirit" (KJV). Christ condemned sin in the flesh. Our sinful nature is never said to be forgiven. It is condemned. It is the sins that we have committed that are forgiven. If you are feeling condemned, then you need to know that it is not from God. Why? God does not condemn us. The Holy Spirit will convict, but it does not condemn.

When condemnation comes upon you, then you need to be aware of where that spirit comes from. It comes from Satan. Now that you know that condemnation is not from God, why are you allowing people to condemn you? Why are you letting people hold things over your head? Why are you allowing people, circumstances, situations, and your past to hold you hostage? I need to inform you that people are not holding you hostage. Circumstances are not holding you hostage. Neither are situations holding you hostage. It is a spirit operating within that individual. Ephesians 6:12 states, "For we wrestle not against flesh and blood, but against principalities, against powers, against rulers of the darkness of this world, against spiritual wickedness in high places" (KJV).

You see, if you are in Christ, you have been forgiven. Your past is behind you! People, circumstances, situations, and your past may make you feel condemned to hold you down. Sometimes, people may want to oppress you. However, if you are in Christ, you are free, and whom the Son sets free is free indeed. You have been redeemed. Why? Jesus paid it all.

WILL YOU BE READY WHEN JESUS COMES?

Text: Matthew 24:3–14, 23–24, 42–44
Author: Matthew (called Levi, son of Alpheaus and brother of James)
Date and place: Written in Judah traditionally in AD 37.

Background

VERSES 3–14 OF Matthew chapter 24 deal with the first half of the tribulation. Here, we see there were three questions asked by the disciples to Jesus. They presented these questions to Jesus after He crossed over to the Mount of Olives. They asked the questions privately.

> Question no. 1: When would these things happen? These things that they were referring to were when the temple would be destroyed.

> Question no. 2: What would be the sign of His coming? Here, they wanted to know what supernatural event would precede His return to earth to set up His kingdom.

> Question no. 3: What would be the sign of the end of the age? This is referring to immediately prior to His glorious reign.

In verses 23–26 of the same chapter, we see there is a warning about the false messiah and false prophets. We have been advised not to believe the reports about secret advents or local advents. If someone comes and tells you that they see Christ outside, over, or in a certain place, you are not to believe that. Just because a person performs a miracle does not mean that he is a follower of Jesus Christ. Just because a person comes with the Word all the time and performing signs and wonders does not make him a prophet from God. Do not be deceived. Do not keep running behind men or women you meet because they say that they are prophets. Do not be tossed to and fro because a person tells you what you want to hear.

Jesus said in His word, "That they shall deceive the very elect." A prophet should not be coming to teach you how to prophesy. This is something that is caught, not taught.

Elijah's mantle fell on Elisha. We see that in 2 Kings 2:9–14, Elijah asked Elisha what he wanted, and Elisha responded by saying that he wanted a double portion of his spirit. Elijah then responded by saying, "You ask a hard thing, but if you see me when I go up."

From this time forward, Elisha would not leave Elijah's side. He saw when Elijah was taken up. His mantle fell down, and Elisha took the mantle up. Elijah did not teach Elisha how to prophesy. There was a school of prophets. However, this is not what was taught. We also see they were not prophesying houses and cars.

Verses 42–44 further go on to remind us that because no man knows the day or hour, we ought to watch. Stay awake spiritually. Be ready. Live each day as if it is your last day. The old saints used to say, "Don't let Him catch you with your work undone." Work while it is day. For when night comes, no man can work. These are the questions I must ask: Will you be ready when Jesus comes? What will He find you doing when He returns?

I need to let you know that Jesus will be coming back one day. However, nobody knows when. We have to make sure that we are ready for his return.

It is time to love like we have never loved before, pray like we have never prayed before, live like we have never lived before, fast like we have never fasted before, and minister like we have never ministered before. Visit the sick more than ever. Try to win as many souls for the kingdom as we can. Keep our Savior Jesus lifted up. Find out what it is that Jesus wants each and every one of us to do, and do it. Live for Jesus. Just be ready when He comes.

WAKE UP

Text: Matthew 22:42–44, 25:1–5, 13
Author: Matthew (called Levi, son of Alpheus and brother of James)
Date and place: Written in Judah traditionally in AD 37

Background

IN MATTHEW 24:42–44, we see a command. Here, it refers to the coming of Christ, which will be sudden.

Matthew 25:1–6 and 13 once again refer to being watchful. The parable was about ten virgins who were not Christians. They were friends of a certain girl that got married over 1,900 years ago. Five were wise, and five were foolish. According to the text, we see that the foolish did not take enough extra oil for their lamps. The wise, on the other hand, took extra oil for their lamps. The text states that all ten fell asleep. They tarried, slumbered, and slept.

According to Finis Jennings Dake, Jewish weddings are celebrated at night. This wedding started at the rise of the evening star. This particular wedding started late because the bridegroom was late. He states that it is customary for the bridegroom's friends to begin crying from the home of the bridegroom, "Behold, the bridegroom cometh." This was done along the route, and people would take up joyous cries until it would get near the home of the bride that it would wake up the sleepy ones. The duty of the ones chosen by the bride was to go out and welcome the bridegroom.

Verse 13 warns us to watch because "ye know neither the day nor the hour whether the Son of man cometh." Jesus is coming back one day. Nobody knows when. Nobody knows the day or the hour. Wake up; get up. You have fallen asleep. Spiritually, you have fallen asleep. Do not let Him catch you sleeping. Are you preparing for His great return? Live, love, laugh, enjoy life, but live for Jesus. Live each day as if it is your last day. The church has fallen asleep. Look at everything going on in the world around us. We are allowing any- and everything to go on. We see wayward children, corrupt officers and politicians, gay/lesbian marriages, Christian marriages falling apart, competition in the body of Christ, people playing church, church fights, church splits, church shootings, and massive school shootings. Wake up, body of Christ.

We see the ten virgins tarried, slumbered, and slept. *Tarry* is defined by *Webster's Dictionary* as "to delay or be tardy doing, to linger in expectation." *Webster* defines *slumber* as "to sleep lightly, slothful, to lie dormant, or latent." Finally, it defines *sleep* as "a natural periodic suspension of consciousness during which the powers of the body are restored, a state of torpid inactivity."

Do not get laid back in the things of God spiritually. Wake up. Jesus is coming back one day. Wake up.

THE EARTH IS THE LORD'S

Text: Psalm 24
Author: David (first Psalm of God, a Psalm of David, God's right to the Earth)

THE EARTH IS the Lord's. God created the earth, and because He created the earth, it belongs to Him. It is now in rebellion against Him, being dominated by Satan and evil forces. However, the earth and everything in it belongs to God. McDonald pointed out that "The earth is the Lord's" is a statement of divine ownership and Christ's full right to reign. It is God who made the world. It is He who gathered the waters together in one place. It is He who made dry land appear. He is coming back one day to claim what belongs to Him.

Who shall ascend into the hill of the Lord? Who shall stand in His holy place? In other words, who will enter the kingdom and enjoy the thousand-year reign of peace and prosperity? Here, it talks about the character of God's people.

John 3:5 says, "Jesus answered, verily, verily, I say unto thee, except a man be born of water and of the spirit he cannot enter into the kingdom of God."

Godlike character is developed as a result of being born again. There are four qualifications for eternal life listed by Finis Jennings Dake:

1. He that has clean hands (Psalms 24:4, 15:1–5).
2. He that has a pure heart (Psalms 24:4, 51:7; Malachi 3:2–3; Matthew 5:8; John 15:3).
3. He that has not exalted his soul to vanity of idols and sin (Psalm 24:4; 1 Corinthians 6:9–11, 5:19–21; Hebrew 12:14).
4. He that is truthful (Psalm 24:4; Revelation 21:8).

WHAT KIND OF LEGACY ARE YOU LEAVING BEHIND?

Text: Ephesians 4:1
Author: Paul
Date and time: Written from Rome in AD 64 and was sent by Tychicus along with Colossians and Philemon. It is the most impersonal of Paul's Epistles.

Background

HERE, WE SEE that Paul is appealing to us to walk worthy of the vacation wherewith we are called. He identifies himself as a prisoner of the Lord. When a person is in prison, they are confined. What Paul is saying here is that he is a prisoner of the Lord. In other words, he is being faithful to the Lord. He is being obedient to the Lord. He is sold out for the Lord. Paul is devoted to the Lord, not to the world or anything else. How many of us can say that we are faithful and sold out for the Lord? Paul said, "I beseech you."

Beseech, according to *Webster's Dictionary* means "to request earnestly, make supplication."

According to Finis Jennis Dake, there were six exhortations to the Ephesians. The first exhortation is to walk worthy of your calling. The second exhortation that was given was to walk in all lowliness or humility of mind. The third exhortation states to walk in meekness. The fourth exhortation states to walk in humility.

Next, he stated to forbear one another in love. Finally, the last exhortation to the Ephesians was to endeavor to keep the unity of the spirit in a bond of peace.

Chapters 1–3 deal with the Christian calling. Our exalted standing in Christ calls for corresponding godly conduct. Ephesians moves from the heavenlies in chapters 1–3 to the local church, at home, and to general society in chapters 4–6.

As Stott pointed out, we must cultivate unity in the church, purity in our personal lives, harmony in our homes, and stability in our combat with the powers of evil. The word *walk* is found seven times in this letter. It is describing a person's lifestyle, worthy walk, and a walk that reflects a Christian, a walk that reflects a member of the body of Christ.

How is your walk? Did you know that someone is always watching the way that you walk? It may be an adult, it may be a child, it may be someone who is saved, or it may be someone that is unsaved. When a person sees you, what do they see? How are you carrying yourself? I understand now what my mother meant when she used to say to me to class myself and that we are judged by the company that we keep.

What kind of legacy do you want to leave behind? How is your character? Are you walking in great integrity? These are the questions that we all need to ask ourselves. These things really do matter. Are you walking in lowliness? In other words, are you walking in genuine humility that comes from association with the Lord who makes us conscious of who we are and enables us to esteem others better than ourselves? Are we walking in gentleness? Do we have an attitude that submits to God's dealing without rebellion or to man's unkindness without retaliation? Are we walking in long-suffering? Do we have an even disposition and spirit of patience under prolonged provocation? Are we bearing one another in love? Are we making allowance for the faults and failures of others or their differing personalities, abilities, and temperaments? Are you faithful to the Lord? Are you obedient to the Lord? Have you made up your mind that no matter what may come, you are sold out for Jesus?

I want to do what God wants me to do. I am going to walk upright. I am going to live a life that is pleasing in His sight. Being faithful to man is okay, but being faithful to God is the most important. I found out that man cannot save me. Man cannot heal me. Man and things cannot deliver me. Only Jesus can. I want to make sure that my walk lines up with His purpose. Not my will, but "Thy will [His will] be done." Money comes, and money goes. People come, and people go. Material things come, and material things go. Matthew 24:35 says, "Heaven and earth will pass away, but my words will not pass away" (KJV).

If it looks like I am getting off the path that God has ordained for me, I know how to call on His name. I want to make sure that I am leaving a good legacy behind.

EVERY KNEE SHALL BOW

Text: Romans 14:10–13
Author: Paul
Date and time: About AD 57 from Corinth as Paul was preparing for his visit to Jerusalem.

History

WHY DO YOU judge your brother? Here, the verse talks about the weak judging the strong for practicing liberty. (Eating meat and refraining from keeping special days.) Where the spirit of the Lord is, there is liberty (freedom), not bondage. We know that Christ is Lord of all.

William McDonald stated that "none of us liveth to himself, and no man dieth to himself." For whether we live, we live unto the Lord; and whether we die, we die unto the Lord. Whether we live, therefore, or die, we are the Lord's. For to this end, Christ—dead and risen and revived—said that He might be Lord both of the dead and living. He further goes on to say that we live or die in service to the Lord. Our purpose in life is to please God. Everything was created by God and for God.

Whether we are strong or weak, we belong to the Lord. We have no right—strong or weak—to look down on one another. We both have to stand before the judgment seat. Jesus said that "every knee shall bow to me and every tongue shall confess to God." Everyone will acknowledge His majesty by confessing to

Him as Lord. It is not a matter of who they are. It does not matter how much money one has. It does not matter what background an individual came from. It does not matter what an individual believes. One day, every knee will have to bow and every tongue will confess to Jesus Christ as Lord.

Matthew 10:32–33 states, "Whoever acknowledges me before men I also will acknowledge him before my father in heaven. But whoever, disowns me before men, I will disown him before my father in heaven" (KJV). I want to hear Him say, "Well done." We got to give an account for our actions.

LET THIS MIND BE IN YOU

Text: Philippians 2:5
Author: Apostle Paul
Date and time: Uncertain (probably written from Rome in AD 60–64).

HERE, WE SEE that we have been commanded to let this mind be in us, which was also in Christ Jesus. According to *Webster's Dictionary*, *mind* is defined as "conscious or awareness of being; the intellect that comprises such elements as memory, original thought, and emotion; the ability to think, to notice, or give heed to be concerned about." This is a personal statement. The apostle Paul stated in his teaching, "Let this mind be in you, which was also in Christ Jesus."

The commentator listed seven steps in Christ's humiliation:

1. He was consecrated to be humble. He was set apart as sacred. He was dedicated to a worthy cause.
2. He laid aside His divine form.
3. He made Himself of no reputation. He knew it was not about Him. He had a purpose. He did not get caught up in who He was.
4. He took on the form of a servant. He did not mind humbling Himself. He knew His purpose here on earth.
5. He was made in the likeness of men.
6. He humbled Himself.

7. He became obedient unto death.

Let this mind be in you, which was also in Christ Jesus. How is your attitude? We need to check our mind-set. Are we thinking like Christ? Are we walking in humility? Our attitude should be that of one like Christ. It is not about us. It is time to take the focus off us and place our focus on Jesus. Regardless of what is going on around us, we are not to be puffed up. We are not to complain. Jesus knew who He was, but He set everything aside because He knew that He had a purpose. We cannot get caught up on the titles. We cannot get caught up on the material things that we have. We cannot get caught up on the things that we do not have. We cannot get stuck on who walked away from us. The most important thing is that we are operating with the spirit of Christ. Lord, help us to walk in humility.

THE LORD IS A REFUGE

Text: Nahum 1:7
Author: Nahum (from Elkosh—a town not certainly known but later identified with Capernaum, near the Sea of Galilee)
Date and time: No date given. This had to be written after the conquest. No Amon (Thebes) in 663 BC. Since Nahum mentions that event in 3:8, it must have been written before 612 BC. When Nineveh was destroyed, this was probably between 663 and 654 BC.

Terms Defined

>refuge—A place of safety or shelter (*Webster's Dictionary*)
>
>trust—Reliance on the integrity of a person or thing; something committed to one's care.

HERE, WE HAVE the character of God being described in the beginning as being jealous, avenging, and wrathful on the one hand and slow to anger and great in power on the other.

God controls the universe and all its inhabitants. His jealousy is the righteous jealousy of a husband for the wife he loves, not an envy of others' happiness. Israel is the "wife" of Jehovah (see Hosea). When He punishes, no one can understand Him. He is good to all who trust Him.

Nahum 1:7 says, "The Lord is good, a refuge in times of trouble" (NIV). I just need to let you know that there is no need to waste time worrying about those who mistreated you. There is no need to spend time worrying about those who do you wrong. Turn it over to the Lord.

I was off sitting to myself one afternoon, spending time with Jesus, when I saw something that distracted me. Every time I would read the Word or try to study, that situation would come back up again. I stopped and began to pray and plead the blood of Jesus over the situation, and the Lord took me to Nahum. He began to speak into my spirit that He is a refuge in the times of trouble. Then He spoke in my spirit that I was wasting time worrying about who had mistreated me and I needed to stop. Jesus reassured me that I did not have to worry nor did I have to fret. All I had to do was to put my trust in Him because He is a refuge. He is a shelter.

Satan comes to steal, kill, and destroy. He comes to steal our happiness; he comes to steal our joy. Jesus came that we might have life and have it more abundantly. Make up your mind today that you are going to let nothing or nobody steal your joy or your peace. Whatever the situation or circumstances are, you will turn it over to the Lord. You will put your trust in God.

REMEMBERING THE GOLDEN RULE

Text: Luke 6:27–31
Author: Luke (the beloved physician, the author of Acts, and a close friend and traveling companion of Paul)

LOOKING AT THE text, we see that the text starts by telling us that we are to love our enemies. Jesus is speaking. He is letting us know when He said, "But I tell you who hear me. We see that Christ is teaching. Hear, and he is teaching with authority."

Matthew 7:29 tells us that because He (Jesus) taught as one who had authority, not as the teacher of the law. He was saying then and still is saying today, "Love your enemies and do good to those who hate you; pray for those who mistreat you." We have a duty to love our enemies. Exodus 23:4 states, "If you come across your enemy's ox or donkey wandering off, be sure to take it back to him" (KJV).

Proverbs 24:17 states, "Do not gloat when your enemy falls; when he stumbles, do not let your heart rejoice." Notice that it says "when [he] falls" or "stumbles." This is telling us that somewhere down the line, our enemy is going to stumble. That means that they will have their day. With that said, you do not have to help God out. When someone mistreats you or does you wrong, all you have to do is turn them over to the Lord and let Him work out that situation.

Proverbs 25:21–22 says, "If your enemy is hungry, give him food to eat. If he is thirsty, give him water to drink. In doing this, you will heap burning coals on his head and the Lord will reward you." We have been commanded to bless those who curse us and pray for those who despitefully use us. We have been commanded to do good for evil.

> If you see the donkey of someone who hates you fallen down under its load do not leave it there; be sure you help him with it.
>
> —Exodus 23:5 (NIV)

> But I tell you, love your enemies and pray for those who persecute you.
>
> —Matthew 5:44 (NIV)

> Make sure that nobody pays back wrong but always try to be kind to each other and to everyone else.
>
> —1 Thessalonians 5:15 (NIV)

If someone strikes you on the cheek, turn the other cheek. In other words, respond to the matter out of the spirit. Our weapons are not carnal; respond out of the spirit. All of us are not there yet. I can admit that I am not there yet. We have to ask the Lord to help us not to respond carnally to carnal situations but to help us respond spiritually. If someone takes your cloak, let them have it. Do not retaliate. Give to someone who asks. If someone takes what belongs to you, do not demand it back. Let them have it. God sees it. God knows what they took. They will not be able to hold on to it.

Remember the golden rule: "Do to others as you would have them do to you." Treat others the way you want to be treated. Strive to treat them better. I have often heard it said that if you do not know the nature of a thing, you will abuse it. When a person comes into your life, seek the Lord to find out why. Find out if He did send them. What is their purpose? How can they add to your life? How can you add to their lives? Are you all going in the same direction? How can you be an asset and not a liability? Does that person, does that job, does that situation line up with your destiny?

We do not know what type of impact we can make in someone's life.

WHAT KIND OF INHERITANCE ARE YOU LEAVING BEHIND?

Text: Proverbs 13:22
Author: Solomon
Date and time: With exception of chapters 30–31, it is stated that the proverbs were spoken by Solomon about 1000 BC. Chapters 1–24 were perhaps written by him in a book. It was also stated that chapters 25–29 were Solomon's proverbs added to the first part of the book by Hezekiah about 730 BC. The last two chapters were added at an unknown time.

THE WORD *INHERITANCE* comes from the root word *inherit*. *Inherit* means "to receive, acquire, take over from another" (*Webster*).

The scripture tells us that a good man leaves an inheritance to his children's children and the wealth of the sinner is laid up for the just (Proverbs 13:22 KJV). When that scripture is talking about an inheritance, this inheritance may be land, houses, wealth, prayers, godly life, a good name, and/or memories.

A good man or a righteous man may not always have land. He may not always have money, but he can have a good name. He may be a man of great character and great integrity. Ecclesiastes 7:1 tells us that a good name is better than precious ointment, and the day of death than the day of one's birth (KJV). A good man—a godly man, a righteous man—lives a holy life before his family and tries to instill something in them. A righteous man does not try to live a worldly life. He is not a "rolling stone." Sure, he may not have all the finances that he wants to have to leave behind to his grandchildren, but he has wisdom (godly wisdom). He teaches his children about the importance of prayer. You may say, I do not have any children. There are a lot of children who need mentoring. I heard someone say that parents do not want me to teach their children. Well, this is when you would pray and ask God to send you the children that He wants you to teach, and He will deal with those parents.

The time is now to start teaching our children and grandchildren how to live a godly life. We have to stop pulling our children away from the church and start bringing them to worship. We are the church. It is time to take away the excuses. You know the excuses: I cannot bring my child to church because I have to work, I cannot bring my child to prayer service, I cannot bring my child to Bible study, and I cannot bring my child to choir rehearsal because I have things to do. On the other hand, if there is a party tonight, you will be there. You will find time for the parties. You will find time for the hair appointments. You will find time for the spas. You will find time for the football games and basketball games. You will find time for the movies and for the mall.

Take away the excuses. You know the excuses: that church is not right, that preacher is not right, and that church is a dead church. If you are a part of that church, if you are saved, what are you bringing to the worship service to liven it up? What are you expecting to get out of the worship service? Well, the musicians play the music too loud. They do not have any musicians. They will not sing my favorite song. That preacher only wants my money. *Take away the excuses.* Get yourself together.

At a most recent conference, it was stated that 63 percent of the unchurched do not believe that Jesus is the Son of the one true God. Only 58 percent believe that all faiths are equal; only 51 percent do not believe that Jesus rose from the dead. Take away the excuses. We have to get to work.

Mark 10:13–14 says, "And they brought young children to him, that he should teach them; and his disciples rebuked those that brought them. But when Jesus saw it, he was much displeased and said unto them, suffer the little children to come unto me and forbid them not; for of such is the Kingdom of God." In this text, *suffer* means "to allow" according to *Webster's Dictionary*. Allow those children and grandchildren to come to church. Yes, they need to get the Word embedded down inside them. No, they should not have a choice when it comes to going to a place of worship. This is not Burger King. Their soul is at stake. Yes, they should have a choice in what color of shoes they want. Yes, they should have a choice in what flavor of ice cream they would like. However, when it comes to whether or not they want to go and worship God, there should be no choice, especially if they are living under your roof and have not graduated high school yet. Proverbs 22:6 tells us to train up a child in the way he should go, and when he is old, he will not depart from it (KJV).

I hear the question, What does this have to do with what inheritance you are leaving behind? Remember the godly life. You may not have money, you may not have land, but you have instilled the Word in them. They will appreciate it later. They will appreciate learning how to pray and learning the importance of prayer.

It is in those trying times in life when we look back and realize. Had it not been for the Word of God that was instilled inside of us and had I not learned how to pray, I would not know where I would be.

The Word is solid. We can stand on the Word. It is a sure Word. Sometimes what we need is the Word. If we do not raise our kids and our grandkids, the streets will.

What kind of inheritance are you leaving behind? What kind of prayers are you instilling in your children? What kind of prayers are you instilling in your grandchildren? A *godly life* equals to teaching them the importance of living a godly lifestyle and the importance of living a saved life. Are you teaching them the importance of having a good name and not having a tarnished name? We should let them know that people make mistakes in life but Jesus died for us. It is never too late to try and straighten out our wrongs if God allowed us to wake up. Do not hold grudges; forgive and be a peacemaker.

> Blessed are the peacemakers for they shall be called children of God.
>
> —Matthew 5:9 (KJV)

> When a man's ways please the Lord, he maketh even his enemies to be at peace with him.
>
> —Proverbs 16:7

Are you teaching them the value of money, land, and property so that when you leave it to them, they will be able to maintain it? Are you teaching them the importance of paying their bills on time? What kind of inheritance are you leaving behind?

THE LOVE OF GOD

Text: John 3:16
Author: The apostle John
Date: Uncertain (probably late in the first century)

> For God so loved the world that he gave his one and only Son that whoever believes in him shall not perish but have eternal life.
>
> —John 3:16 (NIV)

GOD LOVED US so much that He gave His one and only Son or only begotten Son. Here, we see that this is a serious love. This is what I call true love. This is real love. Here, we have an example of an unconditional love. In other words, this is a love with no conditions. There are no strings attached. Jesus loved us so much that He died for us. It did not matter what we did. It did not matter what our background is. It did not matter what side of the tracks we grew up on. He loved us that much, and He still loves us.

It really does not matter where you may find yourself in life today. God still loves us today. God does not stop loving us.

Sometimes the pressures of life, circumstances, issues, and situations come to make us think that God does not love us. This is only because of the lies that Satan whispers. Our trials come, but they come to make us strong. Sometimes we may even put ourselves into certain situations and circumstances, but still, God does not stop loving us. His love is unconditional.

> But God demonstrates his own love for us in this, while we were still sinners, Christ died for us.
>
> —Romans 5:8

> The Lord appeared to us in the past, saying, I have loved you with an everlasting love; I have drawn you with loving-kindness.
>
> —Jeremiah 31:3

Who would not want to serve a God like that? Stop worrying about whether or not God still loves you because of your past mistakes. Do not beat yourself up if you do not get everything right. Jesus is the only one that I know is perfect.

We all make mistakes. We all fall down. We all miss the mark. We all have said some things that we should not have said. In fact, we all have gone some places that we should not have gone. We all may have even done some things that we should not have done. When you fall down, repent. Pick yourself up, dust yourself off, and keep moving. Let that devil know that you are forgiven, and yes, God loves you. Pick your head up; you are somebody. That is why Satan is attacking you so much. He knows who you are, and he sees your destiny. He really does not want you to find out who you are. He knows that when you find out who you are, you will tear his kingdom down.

Pick yourself up, and dust yourself off. God loves you. He is not mad at you because of your past.

> But because of his great love for us God who is rich in mercy.
> —Ephesians 2:4

> How great is the love the Father has lavished on us, that we should be called children of God! And that is what we are. The reason the world does not know us is that it did not know him.
> —1 John 3:1

So you fell, and you made a mistake. Repent, get up, and move on. God loves you and so do I, and there isn't a thing you can do about it.

A MERRY HEART: GET YOUR JOY BACK

Text: Proverbs 17:22
Author: Solomon (generally credited with the authorship of a large portion of the Proverbs, though chapters 30 and 31 were found in the words of Agur and Lemuel)

A merry heart doeth good like a medicine; but a broken spirit drieth the bones.

—Proverbs 17:22 (KJV)

merry—Joyous, happy, marked by laughter, or mirth (*Webster Dictionary*).

dry—*Drieth* comes from the root word *dry*, lacking or freed from moisture of any nonliquid substance; not sweet as of a wine; plain, as of food served without butter or sauce; not marked by emotion; boring; unproductive; to become or make dry.

HERE, WE SEE that the commentator stated that a merry heart is one that is healthful, but one completely broken spirit and dejected will develop many bodily illnesses. This lets us know that there are many things that can ruin health: malice, hatred, bad temper, grief, constant worry, anxiety, or fretfulness. How we think is also important. In fact, it is vital.

Our mental outlook has a lot to do with how we recover from a sickness. Let me explain. A cheerful disposition is a powerful aid to healing. In other words, it is how you handle a situation. How is your mind-set and attitude while you are dealing with it? Are you dealing with it cheerfully, joyously, and happily? Or are you angry, bitter, worried, or fretting? Walking around with a broken spirit saps a person's vitality. It takes away your energy.

Here are a few things that may cause a broken spirit: bad news, bad medical reports, breakups, divorce, job closures, and foreclosures. A broken spirit dries the bones. It makes the human emotions out of whack. Mixed emotions can cause illnesses, hair loss, headaches, and clogged nasal passages. Mixed emotions make the eyes and nasal passages water with asthma and allergies, tighten the throat with laryngitis, cause skin breakout with rash, and also cause loss of teeth, ulcers, miscarriages, impotence, and death.

What has taken away your joy? Who have you allowed to steal your happiness? What are you allowing to worry you? Why have you not turned that situation over to God? He told you once before to give it to Him. Did He not tell you to cast all your cares on Him? This weight is too heavy for you to carry. Why are you letting this thing crush your spirit? Why are you letting this thing steal your joy? Why are you letting someone else's addiction burden you down? This weight is what is causing your sickness. You were not designed to carry this weight alone. A merry/cheerful heart is like medicine. God wants to see you whole. God wants to see you healed. A broken spirit dries the bones. Get yourself together.

God is bigger than that thing that is trying to hold you down. He is bigger than that sickness. God is bigger than that disease.

God is bigger than that addiction. God is bigger than those bills or those wayward children.

Sin cannot hold you down.
Sickness cannot hold you down.
Poverty cannot hold you down.
Anxiety cannot hold you down.
Stress cannot hold you down.
Witchcraft cannot hold you down.
Grief cannot hold you down.
Shake off grief.
Shake off poverty.
Shake off lack.
Shake off sickness.
Shake off anxiety
Shake off worry.
Shake off witchcraft.
Shake off that addiction.
You are covered by the blood of Jesus. Get your joy back.

HOW BAD DO YOU WANT IT?

Text: Mark 7:24–30
Author: Mark
Date: Said to have been written shortly before AD 70 in Rome (at a time of impending persecution and when destruction loomed over Jerusalem)

History

SCRIPTURE IS CENTERED on a Syrophoenician woman's faith. It took place in the region of Tyre and Sidon, which are considered to be in the northwest. It is also known as Syrophoenicia. Here, Jesus tried to enter a house without being recognized, but His presence was made known. It was here that He was approached by a Gentile woman who asked for help for her demon-possessed daughter. Remember, she was a Greek, not a Jew.

Let us talk about the Jews and the Gentiles for a moment.

Jews were God's chosen people. They occupied a place of distinct privilege with God. We also know that God made covenant with the Jews. He committed scripture to the Jews, and He dwelt with them in the tabernacle and, later, in the temple (*Believer's Bible Commentary*).

The Gentiles

The Gentiles were considered aliens from the commonwealth of Israel. They were strangers from the covenant of promise. They were considered without Christ and without hope (*Believer's Bible Commentary*).

We see that Jesus told the Syrophoenician woman in verse 27 that the children (Israelites) should be filled first. He further went on to say that it was not proper to take the children's bread and throw it to the little dogs (referring to the Gentiles).

He did not refuse her. He did say that the children had to be filled first.

Let us discern the times.

During this time, Jesus's ministry was directed primarily to the Jews. She was a Gentile. She did not have any benefits or rights as it was pointed out by the writer.

What Is Important Is the Way She Responded

We see that she did not get upset. She did not walk away. She did not talk back. She did not pick a fight with Jesus. She did not scandalize Jesus's name. Her response was simply "Yes, Lord." It was as if she was saying to Jesus that even the dogs under the table eat the scraps from the children. She was saying, "Yes, Lord, I agree. Yes, Lord, I am a little dog, but even puppies eat crumbs that fall from the table when the children eat." In other words, "I will take the crumbs. I will take the scraps. I will take the leftovers. Whatever leftovers fall from Your ministry, I will take it." We see that even though she was called a dog and her faith was being tested, she wanted her daughter healed that bad.

There are some things that you believe God for. God is asking, How bad do you want it? Are you willing to turn your plate down? Are you willing to trust Him? What are you willing to sacrifice? She did not care about being called a dog. Are you willing to take up your cross and follow Him? How bad do you want it? How bad do you want your breakthrough? How far are you willing to go? How far are you willing to go to help someone else get their breakthrough? How far are you willing to go to see your family members healed? How far are you willing to go to see your family members saved? How bad do you want it?

REFERENCES

Dake, Finis Jennings. 1991. *Dake's Annotated Reference Bible.* Finnis Jennings Dake Publishing.

McDonald, William. 1980 *Believer's Bible Commentary.* Thomas Nelson.

Nelson's Three-in-One Bible Reference. 1982. Thomas Nelson.

The New International Webster's Standard Dictionary. 2006. Trident Reference Publishing.

Thompson Chain-Reference Bible, New International Version. 1982. B. B. Kirkbride Bible Co. Inc.

Author's Publications

Woman of Change (ISBN no. 978-1-4349-9720-3)
Cooking Made Simple (ISBN no. 9781627093084)
Gourmet Cuisine Venison Cooking (ISBN no. 13:9781630040598)
Chicken/Turkey: Ya Gotta Love It (hardback 978-1-5434-5355-3)

(Paperback 978-1-5434-5356-0)
(E-book 978-1-5434-5357-7)

Songs

"Reign Jesus Reign"
"A Melody for Jesus"
"Yes, Jesus, Yes, Lord"
"We Shall Behold the Name of the Lord"
"Every Time I Turn Around"
"I Love You, Lord"

www.ingramcontent.com/pod-product-compliance
Lightning Source LLC
Chambersburg PA
CBHW031540210526
45464CB00003B/1084